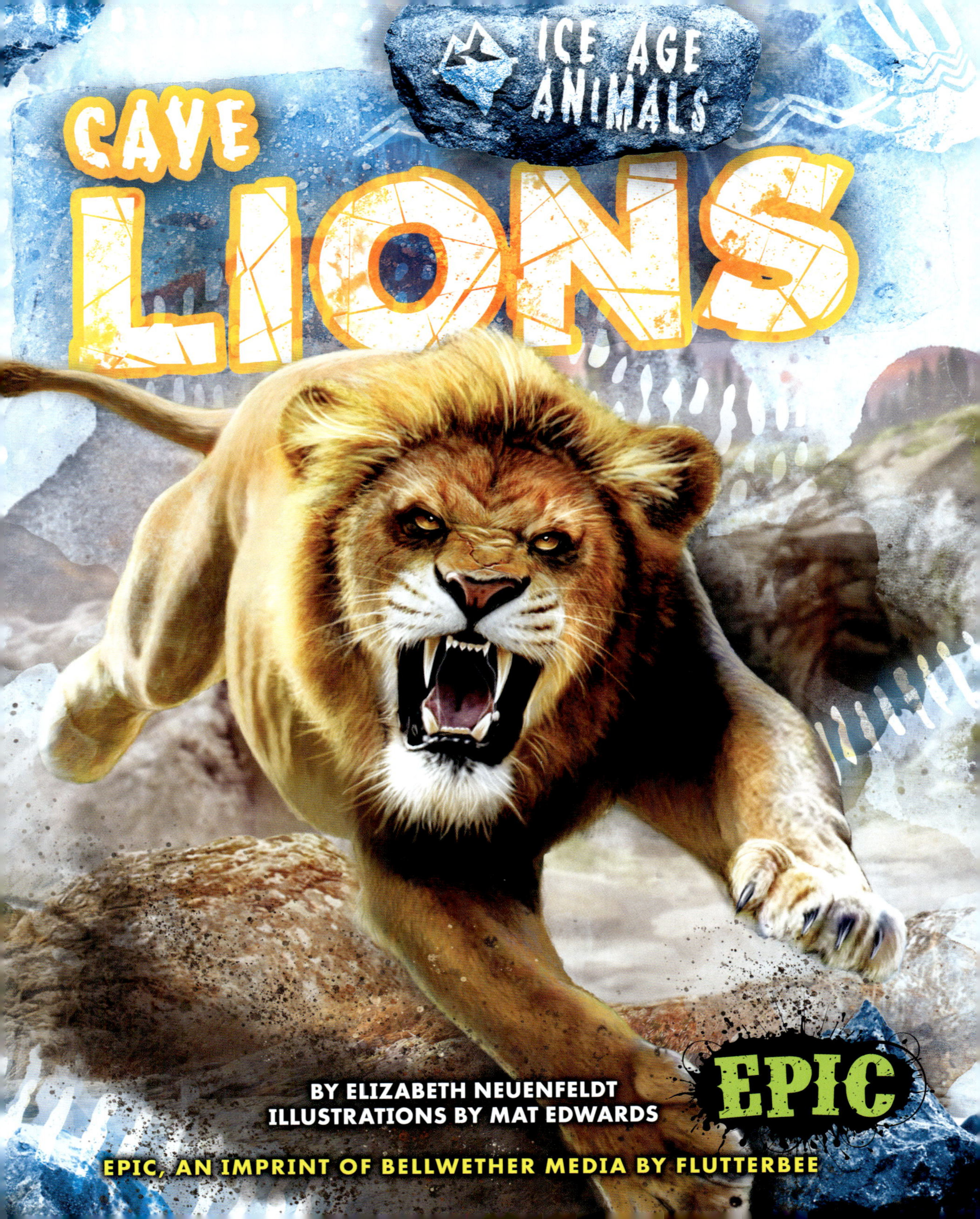
ICE AGE ANIMALS
CAVE
LIONS
BY ELIZABETH NEUENFELDT
ILLUSTRATIONS BY MAT EDWARDS
EPIC
EPIC, AN IMPRINT OF BELLWETHER MEDIA BY FLUTTERBEE

EPIC BOOKS are no ordinary books. They burst with intense action, high-speed heroics, and shadows of the unknown. Are you ready for an Epic adventure?

This edition first published in 2026 by Bellwether Media, Inc.

For information regarding permission, write to Bellwether Media, Inc., Attention: Permissions Department, 3500 American Blvd W, Suite 150, Bloomington, MN 55431.

Library of Congress Cataloging-in-Publication Data is available at www.loc.gov or upon request from the publisher.

ISBN: 9798893048162 (hardcover)
ISBN: 9798893049169 (ebook)

Editor: Betsy Rathburn   Designer: Jeffrey Kollock

Printed in the United States of America, North Mankato, MN.

TABLE OF CONTENTS

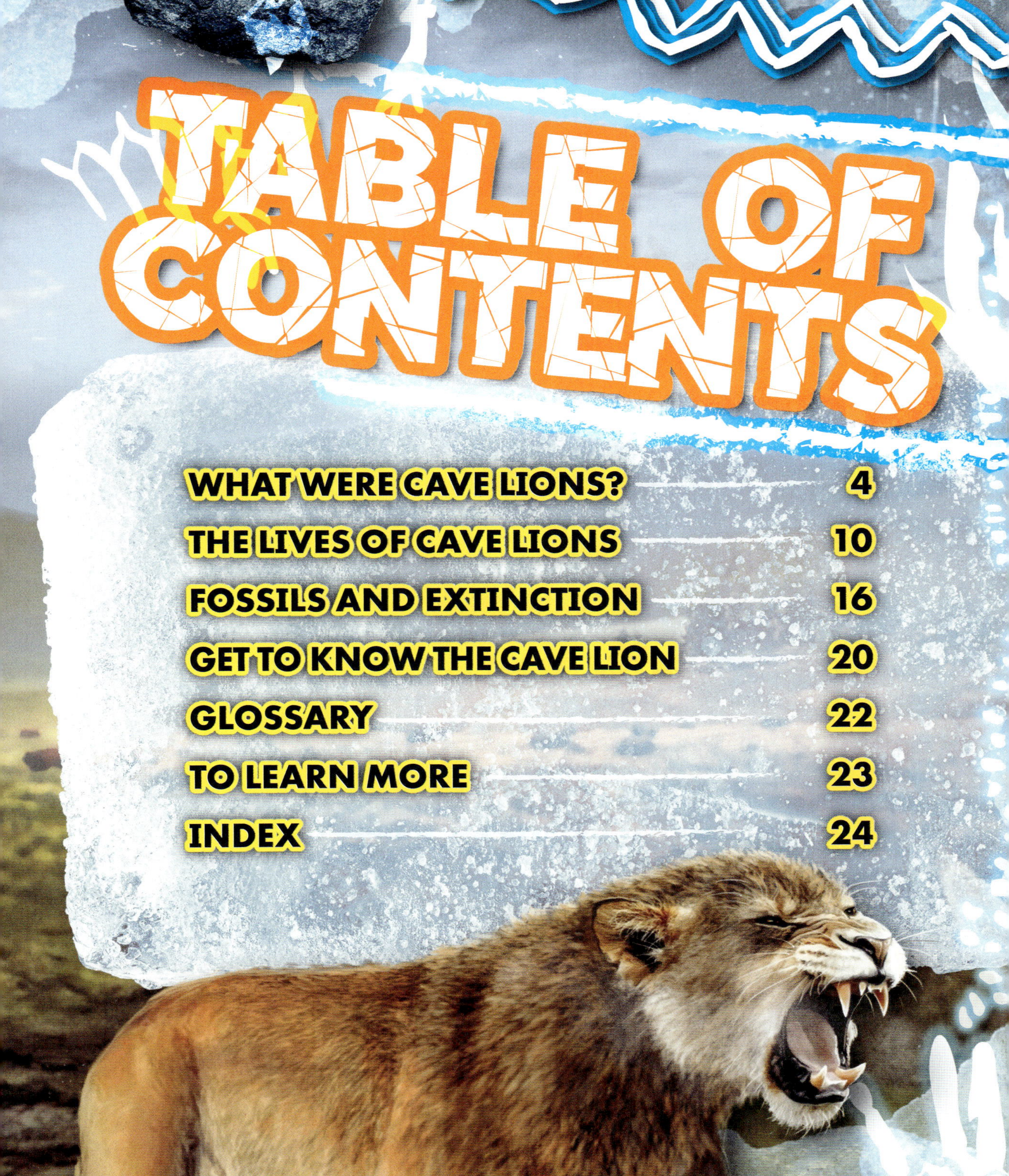

WHAT WERE CAVE LIONS?

Cave lions first lived in Asia and Europe. They later crossed the **Bering Land Bridge** and spread into North America.

They first lived around 600,000 years ago. This was during the Middle **Pleistocene epoch**.

Cave lions were around 4 feet (1.2 meters) tall at the shoulders.

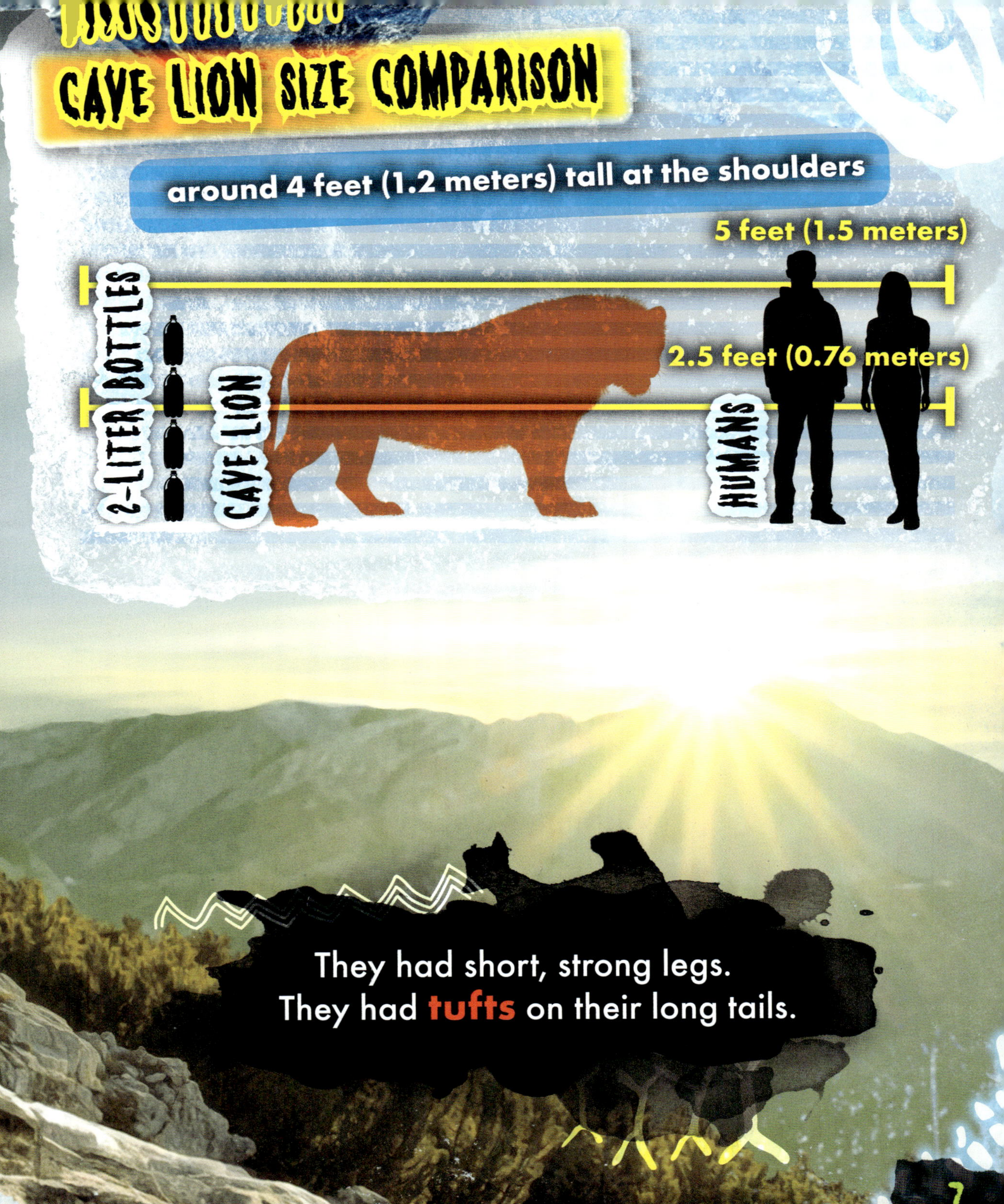

They had short, strong legs. They had **tufts** on their long tails.

Cave lions lived in cold **habitats**. Thick fur kept them warm.

Cave lions living in **plains** had lighter fur. Cave lions in forests and mountains had darker fur. Their fur helped them stay hidden!

THE LIVES OF CAVE LIONS

Cave lions lived in forests, mountains, and plains.

CAVE LION DIET

They were **carnivores**. They often ate cave bears, reindeer, and steppe bison. They likely hunted alone. They may have hunted in groups to catch larger **prey**.

These **mammals** likely lived in family groups. They raised **cubs**.

Cubs were born without tufts on their tails. Their fur color may have gotten lighter as they grew up. This helped them hide in the snow.

Cave lions fought animals such as cave hyenas for food.

CAVE LION ART

Early humans made art of cave lions. They made cave paintings and clay figurines.

Humans hunted cave lions with spears. They used the lions' fur and meat. Cave lions fought attackers with their sharp teeth and claws.

FOSSILS AND EXTINCTION

BEHIND THE NAME

Many cave lion fossils have been found in caves. It is how they got their name!

Cave lions went **extinct** around 14,000 years ago. Their prey was dying out. Cave lions had no food to eat.

PRESERVED CAVE LION CUB

NICKNAME
Sparta

DATE FOUND
Around 2017

WHERE
Yakutia, Siberia, Russia

FAMOUS FOR
Well-preserved cave lion that lived around 28,000 years ago

Many cave lion **fossils** have been found. Some are even **preserved**!

Cave lions are related to today's lions. Both animals have sharp teeth and claws. They have tufts on their tails.

Today's lions are smaller. They have manes. They live in warm places!
LION
mane
smaller body
tuft on tail
sharp teeth and claws

GET TO KNOW THE CAVE LION

thick fur

tuft on tail

sharp claws

WHO FIRST DESCRIBED THEM?

Georg August Goldfuss in 1810

WHEN DID THEY LIVE?

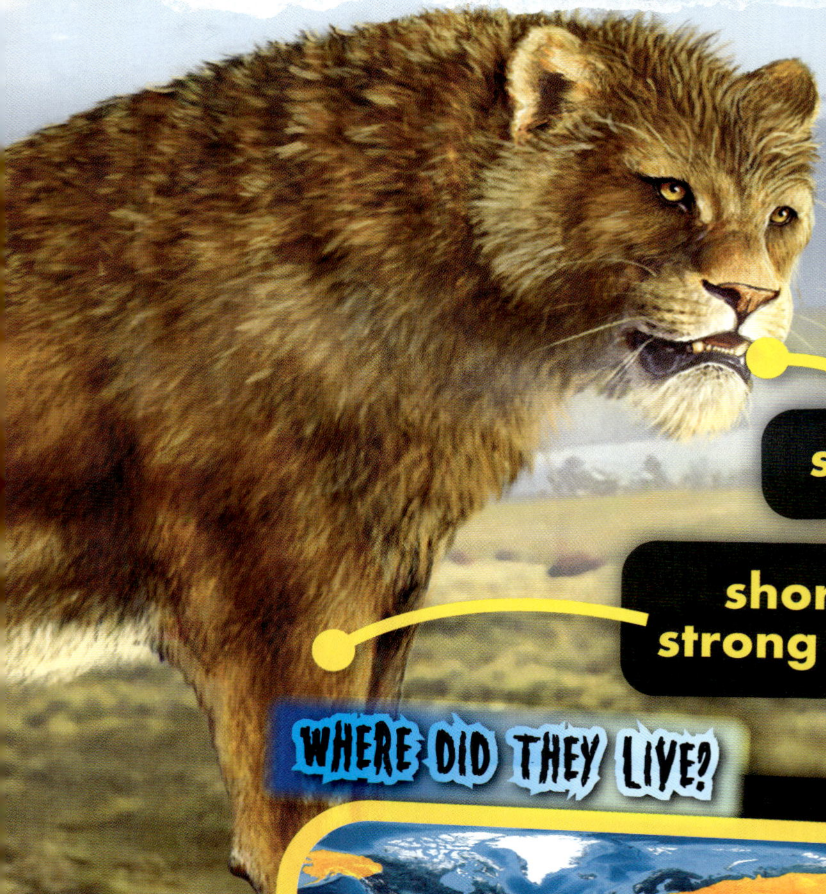

sharp teeth

short, strong legs

WHERE DID THEY LIVE?

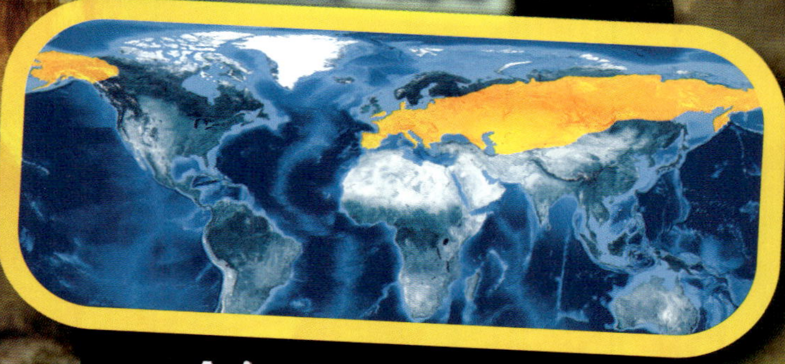

Asia, Europe, and North America

HEIGHT

around 4 feet (1.2 meters) at the shoulders

GLOSSARY

Bering Land Bridge—a large region between North America and Asia that has been partly or wholly above ocean waters in the past

carnivores—animals that only eat meat

cubs—baby cave lions

extinct—no longer living

fossils—the remains of living things that lived long ago

habitats—areas with certain types of plants, animals, and weather

mammals—warm-blooded animals that have backbones and feed their young milk

manes—shaggy hair around the necks and heads of some animals

plains—areas of flat land with few trees

Pleistocene epoch—a time in history that lasted from 2.58 million years ago to 11,000 years ago and included the last ice age; the Middle Pleistocene epoch started around 780,000 years ago.

preserved—kept safe from being damaged or destroyed

prey—animals hunted by other animals for food

tufts—bunches of fur

AT THE LIBRARY

Gleisner, Jenna Lee. *If I Crafted with Cave Lions.* Minneapolis, Minn.: Jump!, 2026.

Klepeis, Alicia Z. *Lions.* Minneapolis, Minn.: Bellwether Media, 2024.

Neuenfeldt, Elizabeth. *Steppe Bison.* Minneapolis, Minn.: Bellwether Media, 2026.

ON THE WEB

FACTSURFER

Factsurfer.com gives you a safe, fun way to find more information.

1. Go to www.factsurfer.com.
2. Enter "cave lions" into the search box and click 🔍.
3. Select your book cover to see a list of related content.

INDEX

The images in this book are reproduced through the courtesy of: Mat Edwards, front cover, pp. 1, 4-5, 6-7, 8-9, 10-11, 12-13, 14-15, 16-17, 18-19, 20-21; Boeskorov, G.G., et al./ Wikimedia, p. 17.